GROWTH HACKS

10 Groundbreaking

Strategies to
Scale Your Business Rapidly

Stuart Ross

Table of Contents

Forward

Too many companies view growth as something beyond their control – a sudden change in customer taste, or a favorable turn in the economy. Many business owners assume that the growth of their business comes down to luck. They have no idea that it is the result of disciplined management practices and the adopting of the right behaviors. Growth behavior is what this book is about. These disciplines allow companies to deliver high growth easily and sustainably, no matter what the market conditions.

After having worked successfully with over 2000 companies across the world, helping
them to realize their potential
and help deliver their visions,
I have identified ten strategies or disciplines that have a
disproportionately positive effect on delivering growth in
any organization. These strategies are what I call **Growth
Hacks**. I have gathered these
strategies together in this
book; if you follow them, your
company will lay the founda-
tions for delivering growth
easily and sustainably.

My story

My story began in the corporate world. I have worked for some of the biggest retail chains in the world including Alliance Boots, which is now part of Walgreens Boots Alliance, the first global pharmacy-led health, and well-being enterprise. There I led the launch of new businesses and groundbreaking initiatives within the company, taking Alliance Boots into new sectors and new countries. Each initiative required a different approach to enable success and scale the businesses rapidly before competitors even got off the starting block.

Let me note that I have a Master's Degree in Business. Although having an MBA is a great asset, it doesn't prepare you to scale a business or teach you what you need to know on the ground to deliver results rapidly. It is this combination of theoretical knowledge and hands-on experience which allows me to develop a robust framework to scale businesses rapidly and easily. The framework I have developed is now called the High Growth methodology which has been used in over 2000 companies successfully.

I went on to run another business, a technology company, which I also managed to scale rapidly within a couple of years and then subsequently sold the business. Through my experiences, I have delivered all the processes, acquired the skills, and felt the pains of what is needed to scale a business. I have experienced a lot of challenges and made many mistakes which I learned from, but ultimately, I've always been successful. This has given me a solid grounding as I developed my framework to scale businesses in the coaching world of High Growth. Believe me when I tell you that you can easily avoid the challenges and mistakes I faced if you follow the methodology I have developed.

In this ebook, I will share with you ten growth hacks which, if implemented consistently, allow companies to experience massive growth easily. These ten strategies truly will result in great impact within your company. They have the largest return for your business, relative to the time investment required to implement them. They are what I call, result enablers. If you focus on these strategies, you can take your established business to the next level. You can scale easily and sustainably.

What is a high growth company?

No company starts out as a high growth company. There is a progression that naturally happens. In the early phases, you think through your business model, you work long hours and sometimes struggle to put everything into place. You have a team; you're implementing and establishing your systems for finance, human resources, management, marketing, sales, delivery, etc., to support your overall goals. In this first phase, the **prove phase**; the test is to leave the company for a period and see if it can sustain and run like a well-oiled machine while you're away. If you can do that, you can move on to the **growth phase**.

You've been building your company, you are running it, and now you have surpassed the start-up phase. You have a business model; you know that it works and you're receiving a consistent return on the investment. Now you know you can step back. Because of the tools you've implemented in your prove phase, you know you're ready for growth.

Within high growth, we have a very simple model that we call the actual "Prove, Grow, Achieve" model. To get a business to scale, you need to prove that you have a business that works; you have sales, you have marketing, you have finance, and you have your people. You have everything working well. Once you have mastered the prove stage, and you know you've got a consistent return on your business — the next step is to scale it.

Now you have a decision to make regarding whether you want to take the "high growth" path or the "scale-up" path. I have found there are four things that set the two paths apart within companies that are moving into the growth phase.

1. You have the right leaders in place with the right mind-

set.

2. You create and sustain high-performance teams.

3. You have a strategy that gives you the edge over your competitors.

4. You're able to implement that strategy consistently.

This is a cycle that is very important to understand. You have made the decision that you want to move forward and scale your business. Now is the time you need to create your team and your strategy. After that step comes implementation, and then you've come full circle back to your leadership. You're ready for the next path, which is to scale up. This cycle got you where you are today, but it is not necessarily going to get you where you ultimately want to reach.

The 10 Growth Hacks

As mentioned before, these ten strategies if embraced and implemented consistently will have a massive impact on your ability to deliver growth easily and effectively. These are not just strategies randomly developed. These have been identified and developed from my experiences in both the corporate world and having worked with over 2000 businesses across the world. I have seen the results many times, and the substantive effect they have in enabling massive growth. Now, I will teach you how you can replicate the same in your company.

Before we start, I want to emphasize that growing a company should not be stressful. To truly grow your company, this is the time to set your ego aside and acquire the skills that you need to learn from the people that have been there before. Take the time to find out what works so you can make your life easier. Business should be enjoyable, but honestly, most people that are in business aren't enjoying the journey.

As you begin on the growth path, start off with a new mindset. You must realize that you need a new approach to be able to take your business to that place where you dream to go next. Now is the time to look inward at your own leadership style and skills. Begin by answering these questions for yourself:

Who do I need to BE to deliver the growth I aspire to?

What new skills do I need?

How do I acquire the skills I need?

What beliefs are holding me back?

Now let's get into the Growth Hacks.

Growth Hacks
Number One

Visioneering

Visioneering is about creating a compelling vision and embracing it. This isn't just any generic vision, but a vision that tells a story which engages and motivates. I am constantly surprised that most companies do not have a documented vision, and the few that do, have not conveyed it in a compelling manner. Let me use an analogy of a competitive athlete. Winners have learned that if they are preparing to run a competitive race, it isn't just about seeing themselves at the end winning; that isn't convincing. What top performers do is visualize and immerse themselves in the future to the moment when they have won the race. They ask themselves questions like, "What will it feel like as I cross the line? How will the audience react? What will my competitors be saying? What will I look like as I put my hands on that gold medal or that trophy?"

This is the process you must follow within your company which we call Visioneering. You will need to imagine where your company will be in 3 years or 5 years and document it in a compelling manner; telling a story that will inspire and motivate.

When you share this story with your team, they need to feel both excited and emotionally connected to the vision. If it doesn't inspire them, convey it in a different way. This inspiration is what will secure your team's commitments and efforts. It is what will move the business forward in both good times and bad.

Let me share an example of a great vision: Winston Churchill could have said in 1940 to the people of Great Britain under attack from Germany *"We will beat the Germans."* Instead, he spoke this great vision: *Hitler knows he has to break us on this island or lose the war. If we can stand up to him, all Europe may be free, and the life of the world may move forward into broad, sun-lit uplands. But if we fail, the whole world, including the United States, including all we have known and cared for, will sink into the abyss of a new Dark Age, made more sinister and perhaps more protracted by the lights of perverted science. Let us, therefore, brace ourselves to our duties and so bear oursel-ves that if the British Empire and its Commonwealth last for a thousand years, men will still say," "This was their fi-nest hour."* This is visio-neering!

Growth Hacks
Number Two

Needle-Movers

I have chosen the term 'nee-dle-mover" versus the term "goal." Goals are binary. You achieve goals and feel great, but if you don't achieve them, you feel lousy despite all the effort that may have been invested. However, even when failing to achieve a goal, progress will have been made towards it through actions taken and the experience you've gained. This moves both those accountable for the goal and the business forward. The results can be learned from and built on. It is for this reason we use the term needle-mover, which recognizes this learning, being a goal with a scale of success. It allows efforts toward achieving it to be recognized while giving its owner the opportunity to exceed expectations. Once you determine your needle-movers for your company, ensure each one has a single person accountable for its delivery, allowing them to take ownership and create a plan to achieve them.

For each needle-mover, I recommend you set a minimum, a target, and a mind blower level. The target level is what will give you the desired quantitative result, the minimum level is the worst case you would be willing to accept, but the mind blower is the ultimate achievement. Your annual needle movers can then be broken down to weekly, monthly and quarterly needle-movers. As you start to drill down on your needle-movers, you'll see how to distribute the work over the coming months and across your various team members and departments.

Each action step that moves the needle affects the growth of your company. You can exceed the expectations you have set; you can meet the expectations or even come in behind. You will be able to judge how much the needle is moving, and how the actions within your company structure are impacting needle movement on an annual, quarterly, monthly and weekly basis.

This sets people up to succeed, at the same time allowing them to set their own standards. Your team members want to be challenged and recognized for it!

Growth Hacks Number Three

Implement with Discipline

Implement your company strategy with discipline. Do you know right now exactly where you are and the progress that has been made in delivering this year's strategy? Creating the discipline to hold regular meetings to allow for review of progress in implementing your strategy should be a habit both for you and your company. This is something that's non-negotiable. Performance regarding your needle-movers and progress in delivering strategic initiatives needs to be assessed on a weekly, monthly, and quarterly basis to ensure individuals, teams and the company remain on track. At each review meeting, use the simple agenda of "progress, issues and next steps," encouraging participants to hold one other accountable. You must be satisfied that the actions that are being taken are keeping the company on track. This applies to both delivering the base business while simultaneously achieving the strategic agenda.

Such meetings also help to avoid "the shiny toy syndrome." As you are growing, especially when in a high growth mode, unexpected opportunities are going to come around, that although engaging, will be a distraction from delivering your strategy. At review meetings, you can discuss unexpected opportunities and make a decision to either pursue this new idea in place of other activities or say "No," in an open forum. Always remember your success is determined more by the ideas you say no to than the ideas you say yes to.

There must also be clear consequences if teams do not deliver. These consequences should be defined upfront when the needle movers and strategic initiatives are agreed on, as well as the rewards when the team members do deliver. Human nature is always at play in your company structures. Managing both expectations and potential consequences will result in teams that stay focused on task because they understand what both rewards or disciplinary actions will result.

Finally, as the leader of your company, you must lead by example. Delivery of those strategic initiatives for which you are accountable, the attendance of the review meetings, the ability to stick firmly to an agenda, etc. are all behaviors you must model.

Growth Hacks
Number Four

Business Mindfulness

Again, I wish to remind you that it is important that you enjoy the journey. There are many parallels between mindful living in our personal lives and mindful business practices. Being aware of the task you are currently completing can alone, bring you fully into the moment. We've become a multi-tasking culture, but there is much joy to be found in existing completely in our current activity, whatever it may be.

The same applies to business in a concept we call Business Mindfulness. These mindful businesses are delivering results through highly motivated individuals and aligned teams that are rapidly taking advantage of opportunities in the markets, faster and more effectively than their competitors.

As a business how do you become mindful? First, be aware of what we call the pulse of your company – this is how your company performs on a day to day basis. Look at your needle movers – are you on track? Is the needle moving in the right direction? Are your customers happy? Are your staff motivated? For any movement in the wrong direction, take action to correct the course. It is so easy to miss something in the whirlwind of daily activity. We can easily miss those taps on the shoulder. They will come back and hit you harder if they are not given attention. Being aware and having the right mindset (being mindful) will keep you on track.

Being mindful is a necessary skill of successful leaders. When you have mastered this skill, you can quickly assess the mood, the focus, and the well-being of your teams and its members. You may be surprised to learn that it can be more important to know exactly where your company is "at" than it is to be fixated on your big vision in the short term. This is another component of being mindful. This opens up the opportunity to celebrate successes with your team in real-time. You don't need to just wait until the end of the month or quarter. Let's shake that dated mindset off and learn to celebrate victories when they happen!

Growth Hacks Number Five

Communicate

Communicate

Communicate

When you are moving into high growth, issues are going to happen. Most challenges will come from disruptions in your communication as you bring more people on board. You need to develop an organizational structure built on effective communication and information flow.

There are multiple benefits to establishing clear lines of

communication within your teams and your company. This will create transparency, ensuring there are no hidden agendas. Clear lines of communication help keep all team members honest with one another thus building a culture of trust. It assures that the company growth path will not be interrupted with situations that arise from the lack of communication. It also contributes to team members being aware of whom to contact when they have a problem or an idea.

As the company communication flow is established, it will also enhance the effectiveness and enjoyment of any company meetings through open communication. They will grow from being dry to truly reflecting the energy and commitment of participants.

Never forget, communication is important to the growth of your business. If you're not communicating, efficiently, sufficiently, and with trans-parency, it will be the source of ongoing challenges.

Growth Hacks
Number Six

Manage Your Culture

Company culture is something that must be managed and explicitly communicated. Start by defining the values of your company that shows up in your culture. Think of your company values as your company's DNA. It is what makes your business unique in the sea of other companies. The resulting company culture is your leadership report card. It reflects how your values manifest themselves in the company from the way employees behave, to what they say right down to how you interact with customers.

You may be asking, "How do I bring our company values to life?"

It goes beyond just saying what your business believes in. It's also about being clear in how your values will be manifested within your company. The key is to first identify each value before providing specific behavioral examples of how they show up in your organization.

Let's look at a specific example. If a company has a value of "Trust," it leaves things open to interpretation. You must define what trust means in the context of the company. One of my clients describes it as "Quite simply, we keep our promises, both to each other and to our customers. The best relationships are built on trust, and that's why our customers come back to us time after time."

Once your values are defined there are four easy ways to bring them to life in an organization:

Put values front and center

It can be easy to lose sight of company values when focused on the task at hand. Values should guide all aspects of business, from the decisions you make to the talent you source, to the way you interact with customers. However, values can't be applied if your team does not remember them.

How do you make your company values stick?

Keep your company's moral code at the forefront of everyone's mind by making it prominent within the workplace. In addition to featuring it on the company website, post it where employees often gather (conference rooms, snack rooms, bathrooms, etc.).

Recruit based on values

Building a high-performance team that lives and works by the company's moral code starts with recruiting based upon values. For each of the company's values, develop a list of questions designed to assess a candidate's character and potential fit.

People are often predisposed to sharing the company's beliefs, so utilizing the interview process to identify people who have similar principles is crucial to building a team that can successfully apply company ethics to everything they do.

Work and play by values

The best way to bring organizational values to life is to model them. Live, work, and play by them on a daily basis, and the values will spread throughout your company.

Actively model company values by aligning them with company culture activities such as taking time off to volunteer together. Most importantly, you have to lead by example. Show employees how it's done by being someone who guides business decisions and empowers your employees to do the same.

Reward and promote values

Finally, promote your organization's values by rewarding behaviors that demonstrate them. Don't hesitate to publicly reward someone for exhibiting behaviors that are in line with the company's character. Not only does this make the individual feel good, but it also pushes the rest of the company to follow suit.

Growth Hacks Number Seven

Get Rid of Average and Below

It's important for us to under-stand that the people who got us where we are today may not be the people who can get us to where we want to go. Loyalty is a noble character trait, but keeping average and under-performing staff around may be what's stopping you from getting to the next level. Retaining an employee that has plateaued in performance can be like tying an anchor to your leg on dry land and pulling it around with you. When your company is trying to motivate or support an outdated employee, it slows you down in achieving your company's vision. You'll need to cut those ties and recruit the right people that can keep you on track.

You must make sure that at every stage of your growth, you are bringing in people with the right level of skills that can upgrade each position within the company, as well as challenge and motivate you as the leader. Sometimes there are people who get in the way of your company's growth. Often, they hold positions that they have not mastered at the level required. Sadly, that doesn't allow someone else the chance to excel in that same role.

It should be a part of your culture that you don't accept just average performance. You should move beyond the people that are average and below average. This should start from the top; the directors, and then work its way through the rest of the organization. It's important that we emphasize that the leaders of your company should always be leading by example, both in actions and behaviors.

The poor performers are easy to address and manage out of your company. However, it is the average performers who are the hardest to get rid of. You simply must accept the fact they are holding the company back and slowing your progress. You'll need to manage them out of the organization to allow fresh perspectives and visions to enter. This quality of employee will drive both you and your company forward.

Growth Hacks
Number Eight

Develop a Leadership Mindset

Today it is very easy to search the internet and instantly get strategies at your finger tips which help you deliver growth in your company. If it's so easy why aren't more businesses delivering incredible growth? The answer lies in leadership, and specifically your mindset. This is the key differentiating leadership factor which sets high growth companies apart from the rest. Strategies are not your limitation; your mindset determines your limits and ultimately the success of your company.

Developing a mindset is about making positive behaviors a habit. It is like a muscle which can and must be trained and improved. The mindset you embrace sets the tone for your leadership style, success, and the influence you will have.

As the owner of the business, you'll need to move from a place where you are not just an entrepreneur but a leader. This is how you get the most out of your team. This mind-set starts from deep within, like believing in yourself, having determination, and an over arching positive outlook. Externally, your attitude must set the example by constantly and visibly seeking out new ways to improve as a person, team, and company.

In leadership, your attitude is your best friend or worst enemy. It's one of the most contagious characteristics of your leadership style. It will cause people to rally around you and your vision, or it will turn them away. The attitude of the leader will be the benchmark for the rest of your company. You can't expect the attitude of your people to be good if the one you showcase is bad. Eventually, you will have to change your attitude, or your people will change their address.

Every successful leader I know has one thing in common- they never stop growing. You can have a fixed mindset, or you can have a growth mindset that will make all the difference in the world to your leadership. The mindset you choose, feed, and nurture is the one that will win at the end of the day.

Growth Hacks Number Nine

Upgrade Your Peer Group

Jim Rohn, the motivational speaker, stated, "We become the average of the people we spend the most time with." This concept applies just as much within a business as outside of work. Seek to master the skill of upgrading your peer groups. Within your company, who is the "A" team that influence your thinking? Spend time with people who will share their insights and wisdom; inspire you to raise your game; who will hold a mirror up to you and show you your current condition. This will set the stage for you to be stretched. You will need that group to support the fast growth of your business.

This peer group also includes your external advisors whom you have always looked up to and respected, such as non-Executive Directors, mentors and coaches. Your current cohorts may not be the ones you need to take you to the next level.

You may have outgrown them; they were fine for yesterday's market but not today's. Never select your advisors on where you are now, select them for their skills in where you aspire to reach. What is their track record? What contacts do they have? Can they coach and support an individual at that level?

It's time to upgrade your peer group!

Growth Hacks
Number Ten

ALWAYS Produce a

To-Stop List

Many of us are masters of the "to-do" list which is never achieved. You often find that you overestimate what can be achieved in a short period. However, when you look back over a longer period, you are often amazed that you have achieved more than ever expected.

There are only 24 hours in a day, so you have to ask yourself these questions:

Are you spending time on your highest value activities?

What are the important actions that you can do today that will keep you on track to deliver your vision?

If you are going to do those activities, then you also need to know this: What are the activities that you need to STOP doing so that you can put your time, effort, and energy into the important ones?

As a leader, you need to master time and energy management. You need to have the discipline to ask yourself the question, "Are you being disciplined enough not be sidetracked by just keeping busy?"

What habits are not serving you or supporting who you need to become? Is this the time to make those changes?

If you are not doing these things, ask yourself why. You will always have more to do in a day than there is time for. As a successful leader, you must prioritize, master time and energy management, and create a space for changing habits.

Change is uncomfortable, but you need to get out of your comfort zone so that you are the person who can BE the leader of a company that can deliver your vision.

Once you have mastered this as a leader, the practice of producing a stop list and changing habits must be instilled across the company. For every new idea or initiative which needs to be implemented, ensure your teams and their members also identify corresponding activities to stop. This allows space and time to deliver growth.

Final Thoughts

As I said before, over the 2000 businesses that I've successfully worked with, I've found that when you implement these ten growth hacks consistently, you can lay the foundation for explosive growth in your company.

As you look back at this list, the activities that are individual in nature are the items that you can immediately start to work on yourself.

With the activities that are for your company or teams, ask yourself this question: Where are you in your company compared to where you need to be? Then proceed in working with your team to produce a plan that fills that gap.

Most importantly, I want to remind you that your business should be something that you enjoy. You don't have to stress about where you are. It is not a sprint; it is a marathon where you don't have to achieve everything at once. It's about taking the time to enjoy your business, to live with excellence, and not allowing yourself to fall in the trap of your business not being fun.

Give yourself permission for your business to be something that you can develop, grow with, and love as you do it. As you implement these growth hacks, you will find their cumulative effect will work to deliver the results you deserve and realize the true potential of both you and your company.

Start with High Growth

Through High Growth, I work with people like you – someone who is leading a company with high growth potential - to help you access the skills, training, knowledge and business coaching you need to move your business solidly into the Growth Phase…. and keep it there.

On the High Growth website – www.highgrowth.com – you will find a wealth of free resources to help you achieve and sustain high growth. These include more than 500 blog articles featuring tools, strategies, and insights that will give you that all-important competitive edge, a mix of videos that give you further insights of high growth companies, as well as free training and lots of inspiration Information about our latest events, ranging from seminars to our unique retreats.

The High Growth Promise

When you engage High Growth for coaching or training, or you join the High Growth Academy, you can rely on our 100% commitment to achieving your success and high growth.

Working with High Growth is challenging, and deliberately so. We will ensure that you confront and address the limiting habits and behaviors that may be holding you back so that you can successfully lead your company into the Growth Phase. In fact, we will set you on a path that results in seismic shifts that change everything.

It's not all about hard work and challenging your beliefs - we'll have plenty of fun on your journey to high growth too!

To learn more about working with High Growth, visit us online at:

www.highgrowth.com

Success is at your fingertips. All you have to do is reach out and grab it.